Rip This Poem Out

poems by

Michael F. Latza

Trindle Publications, Third Lake, Illinois

Library of Congress Control Number: 2015917395

ISBN: 978-0-9968273-0-0

trindlepublications.com

Trindle Publications ™

AUTHOR'S NOTE

Rip This Poem Out

Please put these poems to work. Rip a poem out. Slip
it into a lunch bag, a pocket, a drawer, a magazine.
Fold one into the slats of a bench. Leave one within the
napkins in a diner. Place one under a windshield wiper.
Hand one to a colleague. Have a class of students pass
them out to strangers. My sincerest hope is that you
will enjoy these poems, and that after some time you
will come back to this book and find it empty, that you
will have freed these poems to settle where they will.
But maybe they will never settle. Maybe one day you
will open a dresser drawer to find one of these poems
has come back home to you. And maybe you will pass
it along again.

Michael F. Latza

ACKNOWLEDGEMENTS

Grateful acknowledgement to the editors of the following publications and venues in which these poems first appeared: *The Solitary Plover*, "Cipher," and "Everything Separate," *Howling Moon Arts Cryer*, "Edges;" *Bear River Review*, "July Gambol;" *Willow Review,* "Stage IV;" *Appalachian Journal*, "Sky Swimming," and *Red River Review*, "Listening in the Dark."

RIP THIS POEM OUT

Table of Contents:

BURN BARREL

We have no place
but we are
still so
we stand around the barrel
burning for light, for warmth,
for fellowship.

We burn our childhoods
we burn our search for daddy
we burn the deaths of lovers
we burn our own useless dreams
we burn lost causes
we burn our selfishness
we burn our vitality
we burn old wrongs
we burn angst
we burn love
we burn.

We smolder and
take turns
blowing smoke
upon the embers
stubbornly coaxing flashes
we need to see, to feel,
to know.

Furtively stealing glances
across the ring,
we fade into the dark;
but return to

[1]

cherish the light,
share the heat,
pray to each other.

Gathering, we
shuffle our feet,
slap our arms,
and huddle around
the empty barrel
we must fill.

PEACH

Tonight you've caught me unawares
Wryly slumped within this chair,
A book of poems in my hand,
Furtive smuggler's contraband.
Incognito as a peach
Supplicant for wanton reach,
Take me into you, devour
Eclectic essence treacly dour-
Then leave the convoluted stone
Hard as horn. Dead as bone.

RIP THIS POEM OUT

There are enough flaccid leaves
trapped in books jammed onto shelves;
self-righteous spines staring yours down.

Fall in love with a poem,
an image, a line, a word.
Choose infatuation over indifference!
Make a poem work.
Rip a poem out of your book,
your magazine,
your journal.
Leave edges jagged
for people to wonder over,
"What am I missing?"

Tear out the ones you hate.
Share them all. Others will
say, "Oh, yes," thinking of
something else,
or, "I love that,"
or, will quietly know you.
The next week tear out
another—opposite—
because,
aren't you,
    really?

Slip the page into a purse,
a pocket,
a desk drawer.
Create mystery, create desire.
They will ask,
        "What is this?"
        "Who did this?"

[5]

     "Why this and me?"

as if receiving a grab-bag gift
and thinking...
Do they know me that little?
Do they know me that well?

Such a small
subversive act can ripple large,
like the roiling consummation
of a depth charge.

SKY SWIMMING

It is a high October evening
settling onto the fields,
the clouds tethered in a blue-diamond sky.
Everything is waiting. The pressing silence
rings the noises of movement,
clarifying the gravel kicked up by my steps,
the dog's snuffling, the furtive snap of bird wings on
      the fly,
voles shuffling through the dry leaves. I can almost
hear the sun itself, its white light on the bleached-out
      grasses.

At the pond in a clearing of the woods, I see a glass end
      of day.
There is no distortion, not a ripple on the surface.
I look down and see the cold water, thinking about the
      oozy mud
underneath, the smell of churned up, rotting vegetation
held in stasis. I put tension on the leash and stare, and
      wonder
if I really, really try, if I will it, if I push hard against
      my thinking…
I close my eyes: Oh please, oh please, pushing it to the
      side.
I am stillness, like the air, like the water.
Slowly I open my vision, and there is no pond,
all that is in front of me is
a hole in the earth, filled with sky and clouds,
trunks and branches floating, suspended there, in the
      air,
in the center of the hole, waiting to be touched

[7]

so that they will tumble and drift through the clouds,
spinning away into ether. I am looking straight through
      the earth.

I feel like I could jump right on through the ring,
swimming up among the gold-gilt clouds,
backlit by the purpling sky, and up, and beyond.

I shake the leash and whisper, "What do you think,
      boy?"
But he is more sensibly tied to this world than I,
and he looks around, wondering when
we will start along the trail again.

A flock of geese fly below
and I watch a solitary feather
drift towards me, so light, so ephemeral,
but there is something wrong, there is
a part of me pushed far away,
an unease, watching the feather with trepidation
floating serenely up and up, so whisper tenderly,
until, before reaching me, the air ripples,
and the sky once again is above and high and
      unobtainable,

and the shimmering surface clouds my vision,
and the water is cold, wet,
and temporarily fills the hole in the ground.
The dog tugs at our leash,
pulling me back towards the well-worn path.

PASSION PLAY

The young couple
who live
across the hall
have a fight
about listening.
Yelling, pleading, demanding,
slamming the door...

Eventually
she will learn to say,
"I don't feel like I'm being heard."
And he will respond,
"I hear you telling me
that you don't feel
I am listening."
They will practice,
together or separately,
how to not go
to the abyss,
and it will not take
all of their efforts
to return.

Communication
will be facilitated.

Meanwhile...
Yelling, pleading, demanding,
slamming the door
they are both so huge
in their right

that each has to leave behind
unpardonable obscenities
to guard their side
until
his return;
sotto voiced,
desperate in vulnerability,
pleading into responsive silence.
He pads away
to return, yet again,
gas station carnations in hand
to door flung wide,
so anxious
to confess transgressions
that their words are choked
into each other's mouths
as their bodies press
fresh petals
between them.

Communication
will be facilitated.

IT IS MY STAIN

Oils from my skin smudge the stain
I rub onto the paper. My marks
dissolving into each other
make my presence
indistinguishable:
which is ink?
which is sweat?

The burden of stain
is my birthright.
They pretended to wash it away
but I held tightly crying out.
This swaddling is all I have, all I know.

Eve and Adam were shamed.
Abel and Cain were more aware
of their heavenly gift.

Without stain, could I be angel?
So predictably beautiful.
So cloyingly agreeable.
What would I be
without struggle so divine?

There would be no supreme purpose,
no grand heroic gesture,
and, besides,
it has come to be generally accepted
within the commonwealth.

I can barely make out

[11]

the blur on this page.
I am.
I am?
I was?

CIPHER

I would escape days
extended family busy
each with each
at grandpa and grandma's farm
kitchen table and front porch
bolt through the chicken yard
climb the scrub maple
out back of the coop
and drop from a branch
onto the wooden shingles
my soles slick from manure
where I would scramble to peer
over the ridge, and listen
trying to decipher
the lives of others.

EDGES

Oh, this won't do
I thought
as I ran my finger along the sharp wooden corner,
waiting, at child's eye level
to gouge flesh,
or at least to rip nylons and trousers.
My father would never leave
an edge like this
I thought
remembering the kitchen cabinets,
side tables, work benches, bins, stools, toys
built from scrap lumber
salvaged from shipping crates
in his other life as a machinist.

I remember the first board
that I'd labored over
with his heavy rip saw
and sanded and smoothed
which he used as a finished piece
for a curio shelf
with my name scrawled in flat pencil
along the hidden edge.

"Waste not..."
"A moment's mistake..."
"The right way."
His way.
Hard way.
Hard words.
Learned young, then left.

[15]

Learned old.
Still, I finish
his way.

Today he is visiting,
brought by my mother.
We guide him
to walk the porch for exercise
so that his bowels won't bind up.
He looks around vacantly.
I wonder if he senses
something different...
"I put up a new railing, Dad."
I almost say it twice thinking he will understand.
He nods in his conciliatory confusion.
I watch,
helpless
humbled
as his burled fingers slowly unknot
to lovingly caress
the chamfered edge.

MY FATHER'S GARAGE

You came to me
In a dream last night.
I was in our garage,
The same one where
When I was a boy
I used to pull nails
From old boards
That you found
On the way home.

Only, I was not a young boy,
Angry, frustrated,
Wanting to work with you,
Relegated to the task
Of reclaiming
Used lumber
While you covered the fender blanket
With exotic rings and cylinders
From the DeSoto.

And I was not the preoccupied boy
Who you showed
How to carefully
Back the nail out
And then block the carpenter's hammer
For that last glorious squeal
Of pine reluctantly releasing
Its grip on the friction-hot
Forced steel.

And I was not the proud boy

[17]

Who you praised
Standing next to the piles
Of bent nails and clean planks.
I was a man, and you
Were young as me,
Wearing your
Brown leather bomber jacket
And fedora.

Your eyes were smiling
As you looked around;
I placed my hand on your chest
And said, "Hey, Dad,
It's great to see you!"
And then, fully myself
In the dream,
Just before waking,
"Did you come for me?"

WHY I BUY INSURANCE

It is not that I
Lack faith in the
Ultimate power watching
Over me,
But my strong
Faith in my belief
That rubbing up against
That indomitable will
Will consume me.

RUMOR

Curled yellow leaf tongues
fallen on the yet green grass
whisper from the earth

NO QUESTION OF SPRING

The tender green buds
unbinding my heart yesterday,
teased too early from sleep
by chanticleer sun
are candied with cauterizing crystals
this morning.
Long habit tells us:
there will be new life
and death. We mustn't hope
to know the order.

SEMAPHORE

I passed
a bitter night
with angry exhaustion's
drugged descent
paling the dim hours.
Incubus light
bright white
shook the room
waking me to the world
rock-hard and immediate.

Squinting through rimed panes
I watched puffs of snow smoke
working across
the smothered field
as a Morse Code mink
dashed
from hole to hole;
both of us measuring progress
by the casting
from grave to grave.

TO BUILD A FIRE

very few days begin
with a blaze
the alarm, the jolt upright
the real dream surrendered
to nearly touching
a world—
most arrive
drizzly on
snapless sticks
weeping as I bend
piled high in forlorn hope
me pounding away at the
flint of this life
my frustrated exertion
a fire that I
had hoped I
would stumble upon
and that I
ignore

THE DOOR

You are
essentially
alone.
Nobody really knows
how you got here
but you stand, nonetheless,
in front of the door.
Essential. Alone.

Perhaps sadness brought you here.
Regret, loss, frustrations, anger...
I will not suppose to be able
to expose the nuances of your grief.
I will not pretend to empathize with
even a hint of the corruption of
your heart. No one can
take a piece of despair away.
Not even you.
So you slump
here, up against the door.

Ah, maybe it was happiness
brought you here! There are many
moments of joy if you look for them,
hidden in the small places
we often sweep over.
The quietness within the silence of the night
of a sleeping baby's breath,
the moment after being stunned by performance,
feeling the emotional electricity of
rapt attention before eruption of affirmation.
The fleeting wonder that someone

loves you in spite of yourself. The self-assuredness
of the young, ecstatic in their spiky bluntness
and vitality. The innocence
of hope.

But, probably, it was the next step
which brought you here.
You have learned well to put
one foot in front of the other,
to plod, if necessary, to the next
place in your life, the next job,
the next responsibility,
swept up in the tide,
unwilling or unsure.

Whatever it was brought you here,
here you stand, alone, door in front of you.
And you wonder, what is beyond?
What comes next? What
is on the other side of a turn of the knob,
a push, the slip of time.

This is what is, now.
This is what matters,
that you want to know, that you will,
in time, go through that door. You
will step, you will turn, you will push
and find… what?
It really doesn't matter to me.
But you will want to know.
That is enough.
That abiding unease
may well be the only proof
of God's creation in us.

TELEVISION NIGHTS

I wanted to be on TV
when I was a kid.
My mom and dad,
my sisters and brothers and I
would stare at the glow
in the living room.
Every once in a while
one of us would say something.
Everyone else would shush them.
Awash in the silver light
we sat in the dark
laughing or crying softly.

THE SECRET

Anticipatingly erect
in our stiff-backed
theatre chairs
I sense her leaning
into me.
Countering the pressure
my eyes remain
passively forward,
obliquely obliging,
hungry for the familiar comfort
of arcane drama and romance
while waiting for whisper about
her day,
or the children,
or some coming requirement
demanding my attention.
She places her cupped hand
gently against my head
and discreetly, delicately traces
the whorls of my ear
with the tip of her tongue
finishing with a firm draw of the lobe
between lascivious lips.
Decorously returning
to prim, vestal position,
I am so completely
Dionysian grin
the others must think
she has told me
some delicious secret
shared by
just us two.

[33]

WITCH'S BREW

I leaned too close
over jade pools
flecked with hazel;
solitary apostate,
vortex drowning
I offered first fervor
to the incantation
upon your succubus lips
and in our brim-seeping desire
pummeling cosmic chaos
we rode waves
of fervent creation
until you marked my face
with salt trails
from tears of release.

You knew even then
bourne reliquary of seed
within the temple's
sanctum sanctorum
would float and ride
drawing upon your strength
and protection until,
from the maelstrom of
blood and amniotic fluid,
out of the caldron
of your matriarchal hips,
would come a witches' brew
of another girl-apprentice,
who will learn to conjure up
the tidal powers
of your element.

[35]

LOVE
ME

You signed your love notes
with love for me
or so I was led to believe
by television, radio songs, thin novels,
and hopeful adolescent angst.

Years later, I wonder
if it wasn't a cry:
a petulant demand or
melancholic request.

Or maybe a syntactical statement
of where the object of
true love lay,
and maybe, lied.

LOVE
ME

I signed my love notes
with love for you
or so I was led to believe
by television, radio songs, thin novels,
and hopeful adolescent angst.

Years later, I wonder
if it wasn't a cry:
a petulant demand or
melancholic request.

Or maybe a syntactical suggestion
of where the object of
true love lay,
and maybe, lied.

EVERYTHING SEPARATE

The tepid water in a pan on the stove
The dry tea leaves measured out into the clay pot
Logs split and jumbled in the woodbox next to the cold
        hearth
A blanket carefully folded upon our bed

STATIC LOVE

Your letters I received today, my lass,
They're strung like rosary beads throughout email
and texts upon my screen; I touch the glass
but touch your voice I cannot help but fail.
I hear your call recorded on machines,
we message back and forth throughout the day
just like those anxious, nightmarish dreams:
We run but never seem to find our way.
I visited today your networking page
and maybe later you will visit mine;
we never seem to meet—it is the age,
the most we get is 'breviated line.
Our intimate messaging can only begin
with arms around and laughing, skin to skin.

SHARING THE DAY

I'd like this poem
to be about
a day,
one we shared once.

But I need to work on the air;
not just the subtle smells
green, chlorophyll, fresh cut silage, turf smoke,
and diesel from the boats settled in the harbor,

but the breeze, and the start
of cold. And then there are the
colors in the late sun
which gifted in under
gray skies as if to cheer us
before extinguish,

and the sounds of the sea birds swooping
and a fiddler practicing out of sight
while a nun strides along the quay.
And once in a while an unseen pub door opens
and the music of bold fellowship spills out
onto the edge of evening quieting.

And I really need to work
on getting it just right,
on balancing the scales of reality and memory,
sense and sentiment.

And I keep thinking about sense
of smell and taste and sound
and what colors there are names for,
and what colors are unnamed.

[45]

I thought this poem
was about a day, but
I realized after working so long
and so late
that it was really about you
standing at your open door,

listening to the bawling of cattle
cushed along narrow stone lanes
to morning fields,
anxious to read my letter,
and imagining you looking away
at a day we shared
and that you can't see
for you wiping at your eyes.

But in my diligence, the sun has set
and the day has passed
beyond my capture.

ACOLYTE

There are times when the clay of the present
is no longer enough to hold me
so I sit on the hearth and light a penny-sized bit of turf
chipped off a clump of dried peat. I close my eyes
and let the incense drift me around. A slow, mournful
          air
runs through my head and beyond
that soft whisper of plainsong memory I listen hard to
          hear
the snick and slurp of the sleán and the dead salmon
          thud
as the sod is slung from the arc of the cutter's motion
landing above and behind his head onto the bog
to be stacked for drying.

The workings of the old clock begin to spin;
the chime sounds once for each hour.
Each stroke takes me further into my reverie
until the mechanism stops and silence replaces the hum
but for the movement of the pendulum:
back and forth
back and forth
back and forth.

I took the old clock from the cottage I had to sell;
I could not bear to leave that beating heart.
A clockmaker knows the value of the confluence of
          time
past and present, preserved in one place. It demands
attention. Each week I find the key and wind the two
          springs:

[47]

one for the cog-wheel mechanism, one for the chime. I
        lose
a minute or so each day. I move the hands to catch the
        time up.

The turf has ceased its smolder.
The clock has ceased its call.
I must move to catch the time up.

MY MOTHER'S TEETH

My mother has lost her teeth
and I'm not sure just what to do.
Because I've always known her teeth
when she was laughing with the neighbors,
and with her brothers, aunts, uncles, and cousins,
with her mom and dad at the family parties.
With my father at the kitchen table.
But now my mother has lost her teeth.
I didn't know they were going;
I remember gold fillings
sparkling through her broad smile,
the only jewelry she had
besides her wedding band
and her worn school ring.
My mother's teeth would shine when we came home.
She grew up with dentists that only drilled, filled, and
          pulled.
Her teeth had been yanked and yanked until
my mother had lost most of them.
Finally, she lost a bridge falling on the street, on the ice,
helped home by a stranger.
A new dentist suggested an upper denture
and in spite of her surrendering protests
yanked the last two roots on top,
then filled her mouth with putty,
took a mold to replace the space with
pale straight placeholders for her cracked, crooked
          sentries
which conspiratorially allowed quick passage
for shrill shrieks of laughter.
The new teeth are staid. Disciplined.

[49]

She doesn't eat with them. But now she calls
to tell me that she has lost her teeth.
They must be somewhere in her echoing house
But where? She doesn't know where to look
and my mother has lost her teeth
and I don't know what to do.

LISTENING IN THE DARK

We listen to our transistor radios in the dark,
A fragile audience
Still lying on only one side of the bed,
The other holding comforts
Added to nightly:

Extra batteries, magazines, a flashlight,
Prescription medicines, hard candy, Bible,
Antacids, Kleenex, pencil and paper,
Glass of water on the nightstand,
Tissue filled coffee can on the floor.

Quietly in the now-empty house
Keeping the custom of the night hours
We lie in the dark
Listening to our transistor radios
Distracting us from nothing.

THE COMFORT OF FLAWS

You can see the scar
in the left hand palm of
my leather work gloves,
or the way my garden wall bows
from the weight of years,
or the brown ragged gash
in my car door.
I have surrounded
myself with flaws.

Unintentionally at first,
picking up the detritus of others
for pennies on the dollar
desiring like-new
but usually finding fault,
seeking out the broken
and bruised leavings
good enough to get by
good enough for me.

I run my finger along
the glued cracks
and feel the love
that went into the saving
repair, after the shock,
and sorrow; I hold
a handle worn down from fingers
tightly gripped in the creative
violence of a hammer stroke
from a man who cared
for his tools.

[53]

This is where I belong,
consoled among the used
and nearly used up.
My power slips vitality
looking out from a shell
sliding into decay.
Apprehension, fear,
excitement of the new has worn out
of me. I am. As all these
storied objects are.

My fingers trace the
deep lines of sorrow and love
creasing themselves into your face,
our bodies widening and softening
as life becomes more acceptance
than struggle. I reach for
the comfort of flaws.

LET US BE LOVELY

It is fatuous of me to ask
do you remember
what it was like
when the world stopped and there was no air
and you could feel the elements tremble in anticipation
leaning into the first touch
of lips, the coldness, the heat,
the wanton move in
will she want me
will she want
me will she
want me.

To remember is to imagine
before you found out love
is one person wanting
something off of another,
and before I found out love
is cancered with accommodation and compromise.

Maturity has wrung us out
the need for intrinsic self-worth
validation from another.
I'm OK, you're OK…
but something's lost as we try to be
OK together.
Memory is all in between
innocence and the desire for,
a projection of fantasy
onto our corruption.

So, yes, I need you.
I need you to love me unconditionally
foolishly tonight.
I need you to be as stupid about this
as I want to be.
Let's be stupid, let's pretend
to innocence. And after, as we
drowse together,
as our over-ripe drupe
drops back to earth, together
we may stave off the nightmare
of Hell Hounds clawing
their way through crumbling flesh
to gnaw the marrow from our bones
leaving us bent, slow, and afraid of falls.

HANDS

Absence creates form
in these negative images
peopled by ancient hands,
earth pigments blown
through hollow bones:
charred carbon from the cooking fires,
red and yellow ochre,
calcite, umber.
The cave cathedrals of every continent
whisper to us.

Squatting in the tomb-like quiet
of the narrow space, sheltered
from predators, confounding winds,
hidden from the elemental gods,
The sound of your breathing slows.
You feel your heartbeat. The heat
is your own, the light, what you carry.
In this silence, kinship falls away.
Thoughts drift from the hunt.
The torch wuffles and spits.
You are alone. You look at your hands.
You reach upward, touching the limits
of your space. And desire to
leave a mark, a sign, a prayer
of the hands which do.

Later, others will join, touch, lay upon.
This is God joy: to create
and then have others touch your work.

BONE OF BONE

In all photos
they are holding onto each other,
the three daughters of my son's divorce.
Rattling in the restive hand of fate,
chance has cast them together,
and they have discovered
they are the constant in their lives,
different, somehow, from the rest of us.

At night, in the confidence of flashlight
among the stuffed animals, dolls, and pillows
of their pink and green flowered bedroom
I read to them.
They ask to see their bones.
One at a time, they cup tiny hands,
covering the lamp;
the light can't help but pinkly shine through,
amazing us with x-ray views of
frail bones, dark veins, thin arteries.

The eldest has already lost
some of the fey lightness of
fairy flesh. She waits her turn.
Her older, heavier hand blocks the light
and I reassure her that she has the same bones
and tissue and blood as her sisters.
I have told her nothing
she does not already know,
beyond my surety,
beyond our understanding.
She smiles as her sisters
sweep her up
in their chatter.

[59]

CONGREGATION

He stumbles around
shyly pointing to my office
doorway, inviting
both he and I into the sanctuary,
stammering
"I was wondering if I could talk to you…
I know you taught REP at St. Gilbert's…
It has nothing to do with the interview…"
I have known this man
for one week;
he asked me questions
for a story about a teacher
anyone / someone to spotlight
in the College.

"My wife and I are different
faiths, and it's starting to cause tension."

He has chosen me savior
and I wonder if I
have any answers
questioning why
he sought me out
perhaps because of
the cross nailed
to the wall over my desk
a conscious decision
in uncertain days
when talismans of my worth
and definition were needed.
I chose

[61]

not a crucifix
in this public space
but cast stone, with the Lord's
Prayer chiseled and wrapped
around crossed pillars of faux basalt.

I stumble about my balance
between creed and personal conscience
awkward in my movement from
inner cognition to pontification
readily admitting my reticence
discussing the balance between
marriage and moral philosophy.
"I've heard, love conquers all."

My agnostic office
partner opens, enters through
the closed, unlocked door
and this acolyte rises to leave
in polite, tacit agreement
not to tread publicly
on private matters.
With a few nondescript words
of assurance and fellowship
we part company.

I wonder what my part is
in all of this.
I sneak a look upward.

THE EMPATHY OF THE WORLD

I walked my dog
in the dew cold fall evening across the fields,
a black ribbon of storm
lying upon the far horizon,
lightning boiling within
blood red pale pearl translucence
while the moon rose,
bright, clear, white, and rounding above
the frenetic suffused shroud.
Below, the dark tree line
through which yellow flickers
of scattered home life winked.

I saw my first
shooting star taking
my dog down the road
one summer night.
A faint blue streak
followed by
an astonishingly silent
cobalt vacuum explosion.

In winter's fog, I stopped
outside of the fenced yard
of the twisted skeletal oak
obscurely wrapped within the murk.
My dog wanted to pull us down the road,
but I waited to see what I was sure I saw there.

One evening, Rebel and I watched
a crawfish rearing up on the path,

[63]

raising its claws, swiveling to face us.
We walked on.
Dark cumulus brooded overhead but shafts
of celestial light shone through the rents
as if God or an angel
was going to travel down—
until the sun settled beneath the ceiling,
bathing everything in brilliant coral light,
with plankton-drifts of brown seed heads
floating on green grass leaf seas,
a coyote loping across the distance.

Later, on the walk home,
the cool dark silence closed around us
as I felt, more than saw,
deer dashing toward the trees
at our approach.

Is this a poem
given to me, or just
the world's empathy?

CONVERSION

Who asked
you
to die for
nothing?
Or,
do you see
something
I am
missing?

WISDOM IN DUST

Shame is forgiven
Only when punctuated
By a circumference
Of dropping stones.

WE TWENTY

"Why seek ye the living among the dead?"
                              Luke 24:5

We are embers flying heavenward
from the conflagration.
We are lights in the night sky
reflected in oceans, with you always
between, in our reckless embrace.
We are the flames of votive candles
soothing the dark.
We are the wind tugging against
pushing past your legs
playing with joyful abandon.
We are presents whose wrappers
have been discarded in discovery.

You see sheets covering still figures.
But we are waiting, trembling waiting,
so excited, eyes closed tight,
until the pall is thrown off,
and we spring up, all smiles and eyes wide
and little hands clutched to our chests
shoulders lifted in excitement:
"Here I am! Here I am!
I was here the whole time!
How silly you were
not to see me right here in front of you!
I was waiting for you,
I was waiting the whole time!"

[69]

OCTOBER

it is a season
this breath
this light
this smell and taste
this reminder
everything goes to earth
it is apprehension
not to say fall
it is right now
it will be gone even as I am
writing this
so how am I to
educe for you
my walk in the damp air
through the sienna crunch
to school in the morning
or the moment
at the football game
when I am alone
surrounded by the crowd
stinging wind-whipped eyes
denim jacket pulled tight
or my muffled movement
in the muzzy light
past withdrawn amber windows
as the brief dusk dies
too early

ENG. 121 COMP. I SEC. 42

Every once in a while
within the mote-filled confines
of English 121,
Composition I,
Section 42,
every once in a while,
in the midst of
grandmother butterfly essays,
pet mice death essays,
vacation trip essays,
adolescent angst true love essays,
my car essays,
there is
the student whose high school teacher
let the LD writer
compose poetry instead of
subject-verb-object,
and gently turned the words to harness;
the girl who looked for years
for the father no one wanted her to find
but needed to be found,
and in the crowded airport
she immediately sees herself
in his grayed-out scarecrow features;
the frustration of a sister
over a brother's alcoholism
and they're both ok with it
as she yells at him from the page
trying to break through his denial.

Every once in a while

[73]

the words bleed,
and I am a lone
mute witness
as their wrung wetness
stains me.

STAGE IV

Stage IV.
I hadn't asked for this.
Oh, don't worry,
it's not affecting me.
It came as an unasked for diagnosis
on an insurance form worksheet
attached to a student email
seeking small consideration in attendance.

I wondered,
not about absence, but
presence. Why? Why
would she take my class?
What could I teach her?
And how much time did I have?

Could I teach her to cobble
words on a page? A poem
about colon cancer? A narrative
about a life with an ending?
Happily ever after?

What vision of consolation
would she want to write?
Love? Love that brought her
to this world? Love of this world?
Love of this world for her?
Love that calls her home?

There are too many question marks
in this poem about Stage IV and love.

We should be making bold statements,
making use of concrete images.
How about this:
She is dying. We are dying. We leave behind
tilted stone tablets corroding on the prairie.
Nothing is ours. Not even this life.

But she does not write this.
She writes that she is living.
She is breathing, and breathing
is so very wonderful, if you stop
to think about it. And she does.
With every breath. And in every poem
she is laughing, sometimes leaning up
against the monolith, her hands
placed against its roughness to steady herself.
It supports her, her back against,
but she is looking away from it.
She is taking it all in and giving it all back.
She is holding a master's class
for us members of the novitiate
desperate to be left behind.

SUBMISSION

"Would you rather dominate, or be dominated?"
Short tufts of orange hair overheard
asking studded lips and eyebrows
passing by in the hallway.

I smile at the privilege of youth
who can pick and choose fate to suit
as one would a change of clothes
or a fashion.

Already parceling out
their lifetime allotment of
neighbors, friends, lovers...
obsequious to each other, unyielding, in turn.

I struggle out onto the frozen lake that night
shedding lies and liabilities,
waiting for the Universe to infuse through me,
a speck on a smooth white plate.

"Oh, definitely dominated," she had said,
enthusiastically, passionately submissive...
blissfully unaware
of the deepening drifts.

WINTER DAWN

I rise slowly, stiffly,
this darkest of mornings,
this cold, gray season.
I stumble around in the dim light
from the Christmas strands
pulling myself together.

Rebel is the only one excited this early.
He begins what passes
for his past puppy prancing
stiffened by bad joints and old age,
bobbing his head and snorting,
advancing and retreating.

"Walk? You wanna walk?"
He answers with clumsy
plodding half-jumps
around the kitchen.
I do this for him.
He lies about the house
the rest of the day.
I pull my boots on,
my hat, coat, gloves.

In the pre-dawn minutes
the fields are a muddle
of browns and dusky blue-black.
Frost snow sweeps the hard ground.
Rebel noses fresh tracks
trying to root out the mystery
of what is unseen all around us.

[79]

The coyotes are already gone,
the deer hidden in the woods.
Dry sedge hisses at us
as the frigid wind rustles.
I let Rebel off the leash,
and he heads off
down a game trail.

I do not see the sun rise
at my back, but I can feel it,
and in front of me, the ice crystals
at the tops of the dead sunflower stems,
and the empty milkweed pods
reflect the first light back to me,
a million winking, glittering eyes
as I move along the path.

Soon the leaves of the tall grasses,
the scrub brush,
the remaining seed heads,
all frosted in the early morning
twinkle back at me,
like a field of daylight white fireflies
sparkling with the rising sun
and my shifting perspective.

LANDSCAPE

Thunder rumbles in
from somewhere across the lake.
Hot summer thunder.
I shouldn't be here.
The sun is still brilliant
overhead. The water washes
the sweat of the day from my body.

I have let the land have me
all day. Now I let the water
take me. No one else is
on the lake. The birds, anticipating
the storm, have quieted.
I float, my ears submerged,
listening to my own measured breathing.

The pensive black clouds have not reached me yet
but cold splinters of brilliance
shatter the surface around me
as I float in the space
between earth and sky.

Do you renounce Satan?
I do.
And all his works?
I do.
Do you believe in God, the Almighty Father,
creator of Heaven and Earth?
I do.

The black horizon advances,

[81]

the wind excites the waves,
lightning flashes over the far shore.
I should head in, but I can't
resist diving into the cool
deep. I dive deep
holding my breath in the silence.

WANING CRESCENT MOON

Waning crescent moon
scythes through the rising vapor
of my condensed breath

JULY GAMBOL

It was all play to Chicago kids and Dakota cousins
The week at Grandma and Grandpa's farm:
A vacation at the trough with the cows
Or in the barn jumping into the grain
Or best, driving the tractor around the gravel yard
With Dad, farm boy again, balancing behind the wide
     metal seat.

In the morning we'd help Grandma collect the eggs,
And in the evening surprise the chickens
Out of their perches with the bamboo pole
And yells of, "Shoo-ahhh, shoo!"
Laughing at the tumbled white and red indignation.

Grandma would choose a couple of old hens
Quickly pushing them into a cracked five-gallon crock
Which sat just outside the grassy fenced-in front yard,
A stone weighing down the black slate covering the top.
"Why do you put them in there?" We'd ask.
"Oh, I'll need them in the morning. That's just
So they won't bother the rest of the hens."
And by the time we were up and out, the crock was
     always empty.

One day, after lunch, the drop-down heat of the noon
     sun
Was rolled from the sky by black cold.
Someone said, "Storm!" and we all ran outside
Until the, "Tick, tick" up on the roof gathered intensity,
And the striking sharp surprise of hail
Beat us back onto the covered porch.

[85]

Heaven's profusion poured down in front of us—
Hail the size of eggs bounced and danced in the yard,
White smothering green;
In thirty seconds, it was done.
We kids sucked and tossed the melting ice
Not noticing how quiet the adults had become
Looking down at nothing in front of them.
Then Grandpa said, "We'd better check the corn."
And the men silently put on their hats and filed into the
        black Oldsmobile.

PANORAMA

My travel photographs are all places
and things.
I empty the dusty cardboard suitcase
and I am there again,
looking out at the places
and the things of the places,
and I feel the same;
if I narrow my eyes and still myself,
I am alone, behind the camera again,
looking out toward composition of scene
and I find myself doing this
forgetting again and again
the names of places, or locations,
or what year it was.

And then I am stopped
by a picture of a someone—
I don't know who;
someone who happened to be
walking into my frame,
passing by,
going about their daily lives,

and I wonder, who are they?
I want to speak with them,
I want to ask them about themselves,
I want to make plans to meet later for tea,
or run into them at the pub,
or walk with them,
occasionally bumping shoulders
in the accidental sway of rambling strides.

[87]

And then I am back looking at my pictures,
trying to look into my pictures,
wishing I had turned away
from the sunsets, from the mountains, the trees,
away from historically significant facades,
away from the foaming rise of waves
crashing dumbly on eternal rocks.

WHITETOP MOUNTAIN

Ancient, green-muted light filters
through moss covered, gangly red spruce
falling upon algid, silent, spongy rot
of boreal forest floor.
Unchanged for more than
ten thousand years,
the stolid quiet, cautious respect
of life adapted to partner death.
It is always wet here.
It is always cold here.

My bones, snagged by the chill
gingerly step across the deadfall
to the edge of the gnarled trees
and onto the grassy bald.

From here I can see
Virginia, Tennessee, North Carolina;
musicians who played here every summer
all dead now, passed along their music
as it was passed along to them.

On the horizon, through the mists,
the Appalachian Mountains, and on the other side,
Blue Ridge. Four hundred and eighty million years
of raised stone. Old stone. Life is a visitor
for these mountains. We name and age them.
They will be here long
after our brief race.

Black clouds grumble within my reach

[89]

like The King James Bible.

"All these things will I give thee
if thou wilt fall down
and worship me."

Storm clouds push the horizon near.
A shroud sidles over foothills and distant ridges,
undulating through the valleys between.
Grey, cold, wet flannel
chokes the base of the mountain.
Thunder roils as it has for millennium,
I feel the tremors near, through the air,
nearer up through the granite,
and nearer yet the vibration of my bones.
The temptation to fall down is great.

SCREENSAVIOR

On a day of chaos
You strike the signpost
into my heart.
I say, "You,"
because if I believed in only me
I would despair.

Random Screensavior
like opening a bible to a passage
appearing in some predestined order
according to Your needs, or ours.

Pictures of family and friends,
mountain scenes, valleys,
waterfalls in jungles—
or the occasional forgotten vacation.

Today it is a signpost
in the middle of a town I loved
pointing to a heart-home I had
to relinquish.

And so it goes—
the heart forced to relinquish
miles away from affect
according to Your needs, or ours.

Amen. Shut down. Restart.

PROOF

For our two bodies
constantly in motion
the space between
is only time.
Paradoxically,
if we put in time,
space between
will diminish until
the time between us
becomes finite space
which will rapidly dissipate
when exposed to our
ardent gravitational pull.

REQUIREMENT OF ETHER

My body lies here, on this hard earth,
sheets of nylon, foam, and air
all that keep the ground from me.
Outside my tent, I listen for the pop of fire
breaking the flowing hiss of water
just beyond, and beyond, the ether.

I don't know if it is spending days under the ether
and roaming the wilds of God's earth
that make me wonder if I am a child of water
or of clay. Listening to the yawning capture and escape
          of air
from my nose and mouth, and feeling the daily ebb of
          my fire
always makes me think, who is, "me?"

There is no one out here to look at me.
And so I project a presence up, into the ether
fuelled by the light of one small fire
built upon this banked earth
swept free of vegetation by the dry wash of air
and the seasonal lack of rain water.

Nature calls as I rise to release my own water—
I cannot conceive of an existence without me
here, there, pumping water, pumping air
constantly, endlessly; or is my own subtle ether
escaping, leaving me cold, dead, windswept earth,
extinguished of any fire?

[95]

I stumble over ruts back to my makeshift home. I blow
       upon the fire
embers, coaxing life back into them. I cough, take
       painfully cold water,
swirling and spitting it and a mouthful of ash upon the
       earth.
Standing here, looking upward, I determine to forget
       me,
illuminated by the stars up in the ether,
breathing in the clear, sharp, cleaving air.

But then I exhale my own spent air
as once again light and heat leave the fire
and I stand here, underneath this cloud of vaporized
       ether,
drifting away. I watch the wisp of my elemental water
fade.   A chill creeps up into me
rising from the cold, stubborn earth.

I am alone. I gulp the air. I listen for riffle of still
       distant water.
There is no more fire. It is again, only me,
my requirement of ether, and the unsatisfactorily silent
       earth.

PICTURE, PUFFERFISH, PINECONE

On the dusty dresser scarf
with the embroidered edges
next to the bed I shared with my brother
in our parents' house,
down the hall from sisters' rooms,
are things I see in generality:
plastic vending machine oddities,
coins, combs, candy wrappers,
bent bubblegum collector cards,
shoehorns...
faded chaff of my childhood.
But through obscurity there are
three particular to me—
picture, pufferfish, and pinecone.

The image progressed
within the worn, metal frame:
a class photo with blue uniform,
shirt, cross tie, and oval school patch;
kneeling and smiling in first communion picture;
somber altar boy,
surplice, cassock, and hands folded toward heaven;
then—civilian institutional boy,
outrageous tie and collared shirt.
My senior picture is still
captured within the metal frame
on the dusty dresser scarf
with the embroidered edges
in my mother's house.

The pufferfish was on a loop of sisal,
puffed up, dried out, spiny hard;
it was, for me, a delicate reminder
of worlds beyond our block
challenging me to visit,
oceans to dive into, creatures to see

far beyond my parochial dreams.
David Somers gave it to me
as a reminder of his vacation.
I imagine his mother asked
at some last stop for Florida souvenirs,
"Davey, is there anyone back home
you want to buy something for?"
And Davey, wanting the pufferfish
for himself, said my name
although we weren't best friends.
And, unlike the pufferfish, I don't know
whatever happened to Davey.
The pufferfish ended badly,
crushed in a sibling roil.
I seem to remember it being
tossed about down the hallway.
In a family of eight, dried pufferfish
weren't all that important.

The pinecone I had discovered myself,
odd in our neighborhood,
no doubt from someone's yard restricted tree
beyond my ken.
My mother told me to throw it away
saying that it might have bugs
so I hid it in the junk drawer
at the bottom of my dresser.
Months later looking for
I don't know what,
I found the pinecone still
at the bottom of the drawer.
It was changed; it had opened,
and the seed scales were spread wide
tempting, welcoming fate.
I snatched up the mislaid husk,
pinched, coaxed the brown dry rough,
and found, in my hands, a forest.